Whisky

A Brief History

"Any book without a mistake in it has had too much money spent on it"

Sir William Collins, publisher

Whisky

A Brief History

GAVIN D. SMITH

ff&f

Whisky
A Brief History

Published by
Facts, Figures & Fun, an imprint of
AAPPL Artists' and Photographers' Press Ltd.
Church Farm House, Wisley, Surrey GU23 6QL
info@ffnf.co.uk www.ffnf.co.uk
info@aappl.com www.aappl.com

Sales and Distribution
UK and export: Turnaround Publisher Services Ltd.
orders@turnaround-uk.com
USA and Canada: Sterling Publishing Inc.
sales@sterlingpub.com
Australia & New Zealand: Peribo Pty.
michael.coffey@peribo.com.au
South Africa: Trinity Books. trinity@iafrica.com

A catalogue record for this book is available from the
British Library.

ISBN 13: 9781 904 332 695
ISBN 10: 1 904 332 692

Design (contents and cover): Malcolm Couch
mal.couch@blueyonder.co.uk

Printed in China by Imago Publishing
info@imago.co.uk

CONTENTS

INTRODUCTION

Whisky is undoubtedly one of the world's greatest drinks, produced in some 20 countries and consumed in every corner of the globe. It boasts a fascinating heritage, not to mention immense variety and complexity.

There is also an element of variety and complexity in the way the word is spelt. For reasons long lost in the mists of time, whisky made in Scotland, Japan and Canada tends to be spelt without an 'e,' while whiskey from Ireland and the USA usually features an 'e.' But as we shall see, much to do with whisk(e)y, especially its historical development, is lost in the mists of time.

Inevitably, technology has caught up with the whisky industry just as it has with everything else in our modern world, and it is true that some distilleries are operated by one man per shift, equipped with a computer console. Nonetheless, the days when men with decades of experience turned out a truly hand-crafted product using skill and personal judgement are far from over.

At the same time as technology has been embraced and the making of whisky the world over has become concentrated into ever fewer corporate hands, a growing number of 'niche' distillers have emerged, sometimes operating newly-built micro-distilleries, but in other cases resurrecting 'silent' distilleries and breathing new life into them.

These independent distillers often make their mark by offering a real variety of expressions in terms of ages, strengths, single cask bottlings and wood finishes, but the major whisky players and independent bottlers have not lagged behind in terms of innovation.

Overall, it would be fair to say that whisky has never enjoyed a higher profile than it does today, and the quality of expressions on offer has never been better. Happily, good whisky can now be found in a refreshingly wide range of specialist retailers and bars.

In the pages ahead, we aim to broaden your understanding of whisky, including aspects of its history, how it is made, where it is made, and the terminology associated with it. We also take a look at how it should be drunk and ways of discovering more about it.

But this no dull textbook. The book is published by Facts, Figures & Fun, and in 'Whisky Tales' we explore some of the quirkier aspects of this amazing drink, while in 'Whisky Characters' we turn the spotlight on a range of key figures in the development of whisky as a drink for the world.

Pour a glass of something sophisticated from the stills of Scotland, Ireland, the USA or Japan and settle down in your favourite chair. Take a sip and carry on reading. Learn, but, above all, enjoy!

"I like my whisky old and my women young"
Errol Flynn

"For a bad hangover take the juice
of two quarts of whisky"
Eddie Condon

"Whisky is the cure for which there is no disease"
anon

"There is no such thing as bad whiskey.
Some whiskeys just happen to be better than others"
William Faulkner

A BRIEF HISTORY
OF WHISKY

One thing on which all whisky writers agree is just how much of the spirit's early history is predicated on supposition and educated guesswork. Words such as 'seems' and 'probable' litter the literature of whisky's origins!

Although the art of distillation is documented by the Greeks, Egyptians and Arabs, a strong case can be made for the Chinese as the first distillers, probably using barley and rye. From China the mysterious art is believed to have travelled to Arabia, and by the 10th century, the Spanish-Arabian physicist Albucasis had written extensively on the distillation of vinegar, water and wine.

The Arabians are credited with the innovation of cooling the tube leading from the still head with water, and the Greeks were also in on the distilling act at quite an early stage. Aristotle (384-322BC) wrote about the chemistry of distillation, while the Egyptians were practising the craft during the time of Diocletian (AD285-305).

However, it is thought that knowledge of the distillation of alcohol did not reach Europe until the 11th or 12th century, being passed on by the Moors, or by soldiers returning to Britain from the Crusades.

The first surviving written record of Scotch whisky occurs in 1494, in the Scottish Exchequer Rolls, where it is written "Eight bolls of malt to Friar John Cor wherewith to make aquavitae." However, it seems likely that distilling was taking place in Scotland for some considerable time prior to that, as eight bolls is the equivalent of around half a ton, so the good friar was distilling on quite a considerable scale.

We may have a precise date for the earliest attestation of Scotch whisky, but what about other countries? The Irish claim to have been making whiskey long before the Scots, with some authors confidently stating that soon after King Henry II's invasion of Ireland in 1170 the inhabitants of the country were found to be drinking the spirit. It is also asserted that Sir Thomas Savage gave his troops 'uisce beatha' (literally water of life, from the Latin *aqua vitae*) in 1276 prior to going into battle against the English. Closer examination of the facts, however, reveals that this was actually a drink made from wine rather than grain.

What can be stated with certainty is that during the 14th century, Irish monks used distillation to produce medical remedies, and when Queen Elizabeth I came to the throne in 1558, whiskey drinking was widespread in Ireland. So perhaps the art of whisk(e)y distillation did not spread from Ireland to Scotland via the Hebrides and Kintyre as is often claimed, after all. We will probably never know for certain.

One now retired senior Scotch whisky industry executive says, tongue-in-cheek, that he believes the Irish were, indeed, distilling whisky before the Scots, but that they were using it as horse liniment. The Scots took the great discovery and experimented, honed and perfected it into the wonderful drink we have today. The Irish, he maintains, have not actually changed theirs...

Whoever made it first, the Scots certainly took to distilling whisky with great enthusiasm, and in 1579 the Scottish parliament banned the use of grain for distilling purposes for a year due to a serious crop failure, suggesting that the practice was certainly widespread by that time. In 1644 duty (2s 8d per Scots pint) was imposed

on whisky for the first time, and by the mid-18th century a growing number of comparatively large distilleries were in operation, particularly in the Lowlands.

However, illicit distilling was rife in the Highlands, and a number of measures were introduced in order to curb the illegal trade and encourage legal whisky-making. These culminated in the 1823 Excise Act, which liberalised existing excise laws, significantly reducing levels of duty, and laid the foundations of the modern Scotch whisky industry we know today. As a result of the Act, that the number of legal distilleries doubled in two years, with production of duty-paid whisky rising from two million gallons to six million gallons per annum.

Meanwhile, over in Ireland not everyone was converted to the notion of distilling on the 'right' side of the law. By the late 18th century, some 2,000 stills were making whiskey in Ireland, and it is thought that in 1823 some two-thirds of all spirit sales in Ireland were of illegally distilled *poitín*.

As in Scotland, however, a large-scale commercial distilling industry had also developed, particularly during the later 18th century, with John Jameson and James

Power founding their great Dublin distilleries in 1780 and 1791 respectively.

Scottish and Irish emigrants to North America, Australia and New Zealand carried their knowledge of distillation with them, and in America initially began to make whiskey in Pennsylvania, Maryland and Virginia.

As you might expect, the early history of distilling in North America is as vague as that of Scotland and Ireland several centuries earlier, with the origins of Bourbon variously being credited to the Reverend Elijah Craig, a Baptist preacher in Scott County, Virginia, in 1789 or John Ritchie, who is said by some authorities to have developed a drinkable whiskey distilled from corn near Bardstown in 1777. Yet other sources suggest Evan Williams as the originator of Bourbon. He is said to have been distilling whiskey in the Louisville area from 1783.

Originally part of Virginia, Kentucky became a fully-fledged state in 1792, and Bourbon County was named to acknowledge the aid given by the French government to the 'rebel' colonists during the American War of Independence. Although it gave its name to one of America's principal styles of whiskey, ironically today's much smaller Bourbon County has no distilleries and is officially 'dry'.

Just two years after Kentucky became a state, the 'Whiskey Rebellion' broke out in western Pennsylvania, where distillers objected, sometimes violently, to attempts by the government to tax distillers. The thorny issue of taxing whisk(e)y was clearly not confined to Scotland and Ireland. The 'rebellion' lasted for six years before the President, George Washington, himself a distiller (see p.67), finally quelled it with a force of 12,000 soldiers, more, it is sometimes claimed, than it took to defeat the British! Pennsylvania and Maryland were the heartland of rye whiskey, which, until the onset of Prohibition was the quintessential American whiskey, much as Bourbon is today. Rye whiskey is comparatively 'robust' and extremely aromatic, and changing tastes led to a preference for the lighter, easier to drink Bourbons, much as the big, oily, assertive malts of Campbeltown in Scotland lost out to the more well-mannered Speysides during the latter years of the 19th and the early 20th century.

As in Scotland and Ireland, a large scale commercial distilling industry developed in the USA, with the now silent Michter's distillery at Schaefferstown in Pennsylvania dating back as far as 1753, though the current plant was constructed 1861. Four years earlier a distillery had been built at what is now Buffalo Trace, while Woodford Reserve was founded by Elijah Pepper in 1812. Maker's Mark is one of Kentucky's oldest distilling sites, dating back to 1805, while Jacob Beam started distilling in Washington County, Kentucky, in 1795.

In Canada, whisky distilling is thought to have begun in Ontario during the late 18th century, and by the 1840s, Canada boasted some 200 distilleries.

As large-scale distilling was thriving in the USA and Canada during the second half of the 19th century, Scottish distillers were beginning to experiment with the art of blending. The 1860 Spirits Act made it legal for the first time to mix together malt and grain whiskies from different distilleries while under bond, and pioneers such as Andrew Usher of Edinburgh began to develop blended whiskies. They lacked the perceived harshness and inconsistency of malt whiskies, being lighter in body and flavour, cheaper to make, and ideal as the base for a longer drink.

Blended whisky was soon being championed by a disparate group of dynamic Scottish entrepreneurs, including Tommy Dewar, Peter Mackie and James Buchanan. They were greatly aided in their attempts to secure major world markets by the arrival in France of *Phylloxera vastatrix*, an insect which destroys vines. During the 1880s it caused the almost total cessation of Cognac production, and the gentlemen of England and

the British Empire required something to accompany their soda. It was not difficult to persuade them that blended whisky might just be the answer.

The increasing demand for blended Scotch whisky inevitably led to the creation of a number of new distilleries in Scotland. 1886 saw the start of construction on Glenfiddich distillery in what was to become the Speyside 'whisky capital' of Dufftown, and as the whisky boom began in earnest during the early 1890s, five more distilleries were built in Dufftown alone. Across the whole of Scotland, 33 new distilleries were constructed during the last decade of the 19th century, but bust inevitably follows boom, and before too long over-supply became a disastrous feature of the industry. In 1891/92 some two million gallons of whisky was held in Scottish warehouses, but by 1898/99 that figure had risen to 13.5 million gallons.

The bubble finally burst with the high profile failure of the Leith firm of Pattison's Ltd in 1899, and redundancies and distillery closures followed. The last 'boom time' distillery to open was Glen Elgin, which went into production in 1900, and its architect, the prolific Elgin-based Charles Doig, predicted at the time that no new distillery would be built in the Highlands for half a century.

Meanwhile, the rise of blended Scotch whisky had caused serious problems for the Irish whiskey industry. Until the early years of the 20th century, Irish whiskey was far more readily available than Scotch in England, and indeed throughout the world. However, in order to compete with blended Scotch, some less than scrupulous blenders mixed large quantities of grain spirit with as little as 20 per cent of 'true' Irish pot still whiskey, though they boldly sold it under the Irish pot still label.

Needless to say, the reputation of Irish whiskey suffered, and it had already been dealt a serious blow by the outcome of the 'What is Whisky' case regarding just what could legitimately be described as whisk(e)y. This ended with a Royal Commission which sat in 1908/9 and eventually declared after due deliberation that 'whiskey' – as the Commission spelt it – should be defined as "a spirit obtained by distillation from a mash of cereal grains sacharified by the diastase of malt". This was a triumph for blending interests in both Scotland and Ireland, but little short of a disaster for the traditionalist pot still distillers of Dublin.

Perhaps the most significant cause of the major decline in the fortunes of Irish whiskey, however, was US Prohibition. Prior to Prohibition, more than 400 brands of Irish whiskey were on sale in the USA, and almost overnight, Irish whiskey lost a major market. Additionally, its reputation suffered seriously as all kinds of adulterated and inferior spirits were sold by US bootleggers as 'Irish whiskey.' The Irish War of Independence (1919-21) and the subsequent trade war with Britain also prevented Irish whiskey access to British and Empire markets. While 28 Irish distilleries had been in production during the 1880s, by 1968 just five were still working.

Back in Scotland, Charles Doig was proved correct in his prediction that Glen Elgin would be the last distillery to be built in Scotland for half a century, as the first new distillery to be constructed after Glen Elgin was Tullibardine, which was built on the site of a historic brewery in the Perthshire village of Blackford, opening in 1949.

The post-war years saw the gradual development of a new Scotch whisky boom to mirror that of the late 19th century, and between 1959 and 1966 Scotch malt whisky production rose from 16 million gallons per annum to 51 million gallons. New distilleries such as Tormore, Glen Keith, and Glenallachie were built, while some old distilleries were brought out of mothballs, and many more were significantly expanded and upgraded.

Once again, however, bust was to follow boom, as the

1970s saw a decline in whisky sales in Britain and the USA, and the onset of a worldwide recession which blighted new-found export opportunities. In order to reduce the level of what was termed the 'whisky loch,' many companies closed distilleries, with the giant Distillers Company Ltd shutting no fewer than 21 in 1983 and 1985. In total, 29 distilleries fell silent during the first half of the 1980s.

One significant feature of the Scotch whisky scene during the past half century has been an increasing level of consolidation, and today a large percentage of the industry is controlled by the two leading players, Diageo and Pernod Ricard, who own many distilleries and world-leading brands.

If there has been a major element of consolidation in Scottish distilling, then the situation in Ireland is even more extreme, with Diageo and Pernod Ricard now controlling the entire output of Irish whiskey with the exception of the single remaining independent producer, Cooley (see p.40).

An interesting recent trend in the world of whisky has been the emergence of 'small batch' Bourbons in the USA (see p.41), and a selection of these has now found its way into the UK market, alongside the ubiquitous Jack Daniels and Jim Beam. Although the Japanese whisky industry was only established during the 1920s, Japanese whiskies are also achieving a stronger presence in the UK, and seem likely to be a category of continuing growth alongside the increasingly wide range of Scottish malts, blends and other international whiskies on offer.

WHISKY QUOTATIONS

"You're not drunk if you can lie on the floor without holding on"
Dean Martin

"Whiskey has killed more men than bullets, but most men would rather be full of whiskey than bullets"
Logan Pearsall Smith

"There is no such thing as a large whisky"
Oliver St John Gogarty

"A teetotaller is one who suffers from thirst rather than enjoying it"
Tommy 'Whisky Tom' Dewar

"An alcoholic is someone you don't like who drinks as much as you do"
Dylan Thomas

"The light music of whisky falling into a glass – an agreeable interlude"
James Joyce

"It was a woman who drove me to strong drink – and I never even wrote to thank her"
WC Fields

"Buddhists manage celibacy because they don't have whisky"
Billy Connolly

"I drink only to make my friends more interesting"
Don Marquis

MAKING WHISKY LEGALLY

Considering that the basic ingredients of whisky are always very similar - essentially grain, water and yeast - the permutations and nuances obtained by distillers are truly extraordinary. So just how do they do it?

———— MALT SCOTCH WHISKY————

The process of producing malt whisky has, in essence, changed little through the centuries, although in recent years, greater automation and computerisation in many distilleries has reduced the level of individual skill and experience required by the operators.

Despite any amount of automation, however, the fact remains that the 'make' of no two distilleries is ever the same. While it is possible to copy production methods and equipment, use the same water source, barley and yeast, and mature spirit for the same duration in the same type of casks within apparently identical micro-climates, the result will always be distinctly different spirits. Vast sums of money have been invested in the search for a definitive scientific evaluation of the variables in malt whisky making, but despite the best efforts of the scientists, an element of mystery remains.

By law, Scotch malt whisky must be distilled entirely from a mash of malted barley, and the business of making malt whisky begins by malting barley in order to induce germination. In traditional distillery-based floor maltings, the barley is steeped in water for two or three days, then spread on a malting floor, where rootlets develop as germination begins. So that the malt retains the sugars essential for fermentation, the partially germinated 'green malt', as it is known, is transferred to a kiln for around seven days and dried over a fire or by jets of hot air, usually with some peat used in the furnace to impart flavour. The amount of peat introduced during kilning has a major influence on the character of the finished whisky.

Today, only a handful of distilleries still malt their own barley, with the vast majority buying in malt prepared to their specification by commercial maltsters in large, automated plants.

Once dried, the malt is ground in a mill to produce 'grist,' after which the process of mashing begins. The grist is mixed with hot water in a large vessel known as a mash tun to extract fermentable sugars, and the sweet liquid that results from mashing is known as 'wort.' The 'draff,' which is left behind is high in protein, and makes excellent cattle feed.

The wort is pumped from the mash tun into a number of washbacks, traditionally made from Oregon pine or larch wood, but now frequently constructed of stainless steel. There yeast is added to promote fermentation and create alcohol. The end product of fermentation is a liquor known as 'wash,' which is transferred to copper pot wash stills, where it is brought to the boil. Alcohol boils at a lower temperature than water, so the alcohol vapours rise from the still first and are condensed into liquid when they pass through coiled copper pipes or 'worms', immersed in vast wooden vats, or more modern 'shell and tube' condensers.

The alcohol produced must be re-distilled in order to obtain the most pure 'cut' of spirit that will mature into whisky, and this takes place in vessels known as spirit stills. Pot stills vary greatly in size, shape and technical design, and this diversity is one of the variables that contribute to the style of spirit made.

The product of the spirit stills is referred to as 'new make' or 'clearic.' It is a clear liquid which is reduced with water from its natural strength to around 63 or 64 per cent alcohol by volume, as this is usually considered the optimum maturation strength. Most whisky is further reduced to 40 or 43 per cent prior to bottling, and 40 per cent is the minimum legal strength at which Scotch whisky can be sold. There is also a legal minimum maturation period of three years, and a stipulation that maturation has to take place in oak. However, most whisky marketed as single malt will have spent at least eight years in European or American oak casks which have previously contained either sherry or Bourbon.

Some distillers believe that up to 75 per cent of the character of the spirit is derived from maturation, and the size of cask, as well as its previous contents, is yet another major variable of malt whisky production.

By law, a single malt whisky must be the product of just one distillery, though many different casks of varying ages may be vatted together for any particular bottling.

GRAIN OR COLUMN STILL WHISK(E)Y

Compared to malt whisky distillation in pot stills, the production of whisky in a column, continuous or patent still, as it is variously known, is significantly closer to an 'industrial' process. Grain whisky is made from a variety of cereals, including maize, wheat, and rye, which are less expensive to buy than the malted barley used to make malt whisky.

The stills making grain spirit are versatile and highly

efficient, as they can work continuously, whereas malt whisky distillation in pot stills is a 'batch' process, requiring time-consuming cleaning between each period of production. A much greater quantity of grain whisky can therefore be distilled in any given period. However, depending on the cereal in the 'mash bill,' the resultant spirit may be lacking in strong flavour compared to the product of the pot still. Certainly this is the case in Scotland, where virtually all grain whisky is distilled using wheat.

The processes of mashing and fermenting for grain whisky production are broadly comparable to those for making malt whisky, but distillation then takes place in a still which consists of two large, connected parallel stainless steel columns, called the analyser and the rectifier. The wash enters at the top of the rectifier column, where it is warmed by hot steam and is able to descend over a series of perforated copper plates. These plates serve the purpose of holding back heavier compounds, which flow from the bottom of the still, while the desirable volatile

compounds are vaporised and pass over into the second, or analyser column. Here the vapours are cooled as they rise up the column, eventually evaporating and being collected in liquid form. It is possible to distil to a strength of just below 95 per cent when producing grain whisky in a column still.

In the USA, the first column of the still is usually known as the 'beer still' while the second distillation takes place in either a 'doubler' or 'thumper' still, which is not dissimilar in shape to a pot still.

——— BLENDED SCOTCH WHISKY ———

Although sales of malt Scotch whisky are increasing, blended spirit still accounts for more than 90 per cent of all Scotch whisky consumed around the world. Blending is one of the most skilful aspects of whisky production, and the best blenders are very highly regarded. They work almost exclusively by nose, rarely actually drinking any of the whiskies they are evaluating.

The average blended whisky comprises malts from up to 30 different distilleries, along with two or three grain whiskies, and the blender will choose these to produce a whisky in the required style and at the required cost. More expensive blends will usually contain a higher proportion of malts and older whiskies than cheaper ones.

Once selected, casks of the component malt and grain whiskies are poured into a vast blending vat, where compressed air mixes the contents. The newly created blend is then casked for several months to allow the components to 'marry,' though some blenders prefer to keep the marriage of malts and the marriage of grains separate until bottling. Prior to bottling, the blend is usually reduced with water to market strength, caramel may be added to enhance the colour and ensure consistency, and filtration normally takes place so that the whisky will not become cloudy if water is added by the consumer.

BLENDED MALT SCOTCH WHISKY

Blended malts represent a small but increasingly important sector of the Scotch whisky market. Previously referred to as 'vatted malts,' they consist of a number of different malt whiskies blended together. As with blended whiskies, any age statement on the bottle must refer to the youngest whisky in the blend. One advantage of marketing a blended malt is that whereas quantities of single malt are finite, and restricted by the inventory of one individual distillery, a blended malt can draw on a much wider range of stocks, guaranteeing supply if markets expand dramatically.

IRISH WHISKEY

Irish distillers use both pot and column stills, producing grain spirit, usually from corn, in the column stills, while what is termed Irish 'pure pot still whiskey' is made in pot stills from a mixture of both malted and raw barley. Between 40 and 50 per cent of malted barley is a typical amount in the mash bill. Traditionally, Irish distillers did not use peat smoke when drying their malting barley, and Irish pot still whiskey is triple-distilled. At Bushmills in County Antrim, the pot stills are used to produce malt whiskey in the Scottish tradition. Blended Irish whiskeys are made from a mixture of pot and column still spirits. Like Scotch, Irish whiskey must be distilled and matured in the country of its creation for a minimum period of three years.

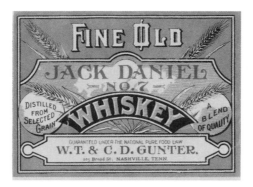

BOURBON WHISKEY

By law, Bourbon must be produced from a mash of not less than 51 per cent corn grain, and is usually made from between 70 and 90 per cent corn, with some barley malt or rye and wheat in the mash bill. All Bourbons contain an amount of malted barley, as this helps to activate the enzymes in the other grains used. Legally, Bourbon has to be matured in new, charred, white oak barrels for a minimum of two years and must not be sold with an alcoholic strength of less than 40% alcohol by volume. It is produced in column stills, with the notable exception of Woodford Reserve distillery, which triple distils its spirit in Scottish-made copper pot stills. Although Kentucky is the heartland of Bourbon, there is nothing to prevent it being produced elsewhere.

TENNESSEE WHISKEY

Tennessee whiskeys are essentially Bourbon-style spirits which undergo a distinctive filtration through sugar maple charcoal. This is known as the Lincoln County Process, and takes place before the spirit is filled into casks. This filtration removes some of the undesirable congenerics and fusel oils, and was first used in 1825. Since 1941, Tennessee whiskey has been formally recognised as a distinctive style within the USA.

RYE WHISKEY

Rye whiskey must be made from a mash of not less than 51 per cent corn, and as with Bourbon, virgin charred oak barrels have to be used for maturation. The minimum maturation period is also two years. With Both bourbon and rye, no artificial colouring is permitted.

CANADIAN WHISKY

All Canadian whisky is distilled in column stills, and in most cases, rye is blended with a comparatively neutral, base spirit, sometimes along with Bourbon-type whisky and corn whisky. Unlike US Bourbon and rye, pre-used casks may be employed for maturation, and Bourbon and sherry casks are regularly purchased for that process. As with Scotch and Irish, Canadian whisky must be matured for a minimum of three years before it can legally be offered for sale.

JAPANESE WHISKY

Japanese distillers take Scotland as their model, distilling malt whisky in pot stills and grain whisky in column stills, though some of the pot stills are direct-fired, rather than being heated by steam coils, as is now customary in Scotland. As with Scotch, blended Japanese whisky is a mixture of both malt and grain spirit.

MAKING WHISKY ILLEGALLY

When you consider the years of experience, the careful choice of finest ingredients and the expensive equipment that go to make the whisky we drink today, it is hardly surprising that when the spirit is made illicitly it tends to lack the finesse of the legal product. As well as the makeshift nature of the plant itself, a lack of hygiene, and the fact that everything has to be done as quickly as possible to reduce the risk of detection, there also is the rather important matter of maturation.

Taste New Make (see p.84) spirit straight from one of

the finest legal stills in Scotland, Ireland or the USA and you immediately realise that whatever complex chemical reactions happen to it while it is in the cask, they are essential to produce a mellow, rounded, spirit.

Whisky produced illicitly rarely enjoys the luxury of time spent maturing in wood, and the result of even the best illegal distiller's handiwork tends to be on the harsh side. Working in a hurry also means that frequently he does not distil his spirit twice, adding to its harshness and giving it the ability to induce a hangover to end all hangovers.

You might have expected that all-round anti-establishment Irish republican figure Brendan Behan, playwright and semi-professional drinker, would be on the side of the illicit distiller, but this was not the case. Behan once wrote "No matter what anyone tells you about the fine old drop of the mountain dew, it stands to sense that a few old men sitting up in the back of a haggard with milk churns and all sorts of improvised apparatus cannot hope to make good spirit."

Yet they certainly tried, and some still do.

As soon as government levies a duty on any commodity it immediately becomes ripe for illicit trading, and governments have been taxing whisky for a very long time. In Scotland, for example, the first excise duty was imposed in 1644, and it is a pretty safe bet that before 1645 arrived, illicit whisky was changing hands.

According to legend, in 1777 there were some 400 working distilleries in Edinburgh. The problem for the authorities was that only eight held licences. In the Highlands the situation was far worse, particularly in remote places such as Glenlivet, in the wild heartland of Speyside, where 200 stills were said to be in simultaneous operation. Matters were only substantially improved as a result of the 1823 Excise Act, which made legal distilling a much more attractive proposition than had previously been the case. The effectiveness of this legislation can be seen by the fact that in 1823 there were 4,563 convictions for illicit distilling in Scotland, but by 1847 the figure had fallen to 64, and in 1874 a mere six.

Not that illicit distillation has totally ceased in Scotland, though instances today are very few and far between. In Ireland, however, the tradition of making poteen, or *poitín* to be accurate about the Gaelic, continues to thrive, especially in the far west and around the border between Northern Ireland and the Republic.

The traditional '*poitin* counties' were Donegal, Mayo, Tyrone, Antrim, Derry and Galway, and the trade still continues, with a blind eye frequently being turned by the authorities.

Nonetheless, the scale is comparatively small when one considers it was estimated that around 3.8 million of the 11.4 million gallons of spirit produced in Ireland in 1806 were illegally distilled.

These days it is likely that more *poitin* is being distilled in cities such as Belfast and Derry than in any of the customary old rural locations, while Irish prisons have long been sources of ingeniously-distilled *poitin*. The modern *poitin* maker, or Scottish illicit distiller, come to that, is likely to use sugar, beet, treacle or even potatoes rather than barley, as was once the case.

In the USA, as in Ireland, a tradition of 'moonshining' persists, and like Ireland there has been something of a shift away from the established rural heartlands of illicit distilling – Georgia, Kentucky, the Carolinas and Tennessee - into the cities. During the mid-1970s, US revenue authorities estimated that more than 60 per cent of all illicit whiskey was produced in urban areas.

But more than half a century earlier, US history had conspired to provide an opportunity for illicit distillers and those involved in trafficking in the spirit to make a great deal of money.

This opportunity came when, in 1919, the USA officially became a 'dry' country under the provisions of the Volstead Act. Prohibition was clearly more honoured in the breach than the observance, however, with 96,000 illicit stills being discovered during 1921, and by 1930 that figure had risen to 282,000. Even for a large country, that represents a great deal of law-breaking.

More interesting still is the fact that of the 2,739 cases concerning illicit distillation and its supply brought by the State during 1923, only 277 resulted in convictions. It was extremely difficult to persuade juries to convict in such cases, since most members were them-selves guilty of similar offences. Whiskey could be prescribed by doctors for 'medicinal purposes', and during 1922 doctors in Chicago alone prescribed some 200,000 gallons. One very sick city...

Some of the liquor offered to thirsty Americans was enough in itself to make you sick, however. Extremely unpleasant, and even lethal, home-made concoctions such as 'bathtub gin', were offered in the 'speakeasies' of New York and Chicago, but the illegal importation of Scotch whisky was also a major factor during Prohibition.

Captain William McCoy was a noted 'runner' of illicit liquor in his clipper *Arethusa*, but unlike many similar figures, the whisky he provided was always the genuine article, usually the respected Cutty Sark blend, hence the origin of the expression 'the Real McCoy.'

McCoy was not the only winner during Prohibition. Samuel Bronfman, ultimately president of the vast Seagram Distillers organisation, made a fortune by running Canadian whisky into the notionally 'dry' USA. Another person to make millions of dollars out of illicit liquor was America's most infamous gangster, Al Capone.

In 1933 President Roosevelt finally repealed Prohibition, rightly gauging the mood of the country and tacitly admitting that 'the great experiment' as it was sometimes known had proved a failure. If anything, the people of the USA drank more during Prohibition than they had done previously!

"When I was younger I made it a rule
never to take strong drink before lunch.
It is now my rule never to do so before breakfast"
Sir Winston Churchill

WHISKIES
OF THE WORLD

Whisky is produced in countries as culturally, climatically and geographically diverse as Scotland, the USA, Japan, India, Thailand and Australia. Although the residents of Kentucky and County Cork might disagree, much of the world is of the opinion that Scotch is *the* whisky, but there is plenty of competition out there, as we shall see.

——————— SCOTCH WHISKY ———————

Both malt and grain whiskies are distilled in Scotland. Malt whiskies tend to be grouped within a number of regional categories, usually Speyside, Highland, Campbeltown, Islay, Islands and Lowland, though sub-divisions are frequently made within these categories.

It is important to remember that such classifications really exist for geographical convenience rather than stylistic similarity. Within each there will be major variations of spirit character, which is one of the factors that make Scotch malt whisky so fascinating.

SPEYSIDE

More than half of Scotland's 89 operational malt whisky distilleries are located within the Speyside region of north-east Scotland. For many aficionados, Speyside is *the* whisky region. It is to malts what Cognac is to brandies.

Speyside boomed during the late 19th century, when blended whiskies began to take the world by storm. The smooth, comparatively subtle character of many Speyside malts was ideally suited for blends destined to be assaulted by soda siphons in gentlemen's clubs and officers' messes around the British Empire. No fewer than 21 distilleries were built on Speyside during the 1890s alone.

Today, Speyside remains home to many of the greatest names in Scotch whisky, such as Glenfiddich, Glenfarclas, Glen Grant, The Glenlivet and The Macallan. Stylistically, Speysides vary from the light, soft, floral nature of whiskies like Knockando and Cardhu to weighty, more complex and heavily sherried malts such as Mortlach and The Macallan.

HIGHLAND

According to historic excise legislation, Highland malt whiskies are distilled north of a line stretching between Greenock on the Firth of Clyde in the west and Dundee on the Firth of Tay in the east. Whisky commentators often sub-divide the vast Highland region into a number of smaller areas, within which there may be stylistic similarities. References to Northern, Western, Eastern and Southern Highland areas of production are common.

Geographically, the Highland region of malt whiskies embraces Scotland's most northerly mainland distillery of Pulteney, in the Caithness port of Wick, and its most westerly in the shape of Oban. Interestingly, although so far apart, these two whiskies share similar characteristics, in that both are comparatively dry, with a whiff of sea salt about them.

Some of the leading – though incredibly diverse - Highland single malts are the complex Clynelish spirit from the east coast of Sutherland, Dalwhinnie, Royal Lochnagar, Glengoyne, Aberfeldy and Edradour. Edradour has long prided itself on being Scotland's smallest distillery, and is situated near the popular Perthshire holiday town of Pitlochry.

CAMPBELTOWN

Once the 'whisky capital' of Scotland, with no fewer than 21 working distilleries during the 1880s, Campbeltown lies near the southern tip of the remote Kintyre peninsula in Argyllshire.

When Campbeltown was at its distilling height, stylistically, its whiskies tended to be big-bodied, heavy, peaty beasts, eventually even referred to as 'stinking fish' when quality was sacrificed for quality during the 1920s. Today, Campbeltown's whisky-making industry is a shadow of its former self, with just Springbank, Glen Scotia and Glengyle in operation, though Springbank remains a classic malt with a worldwide reputation for excellence. Distilling recommenced at Glengyle in 2004, after almost eight decades of silence, and the Scotch Whisky Association subsequently reinstated Campbeltown as a separate whisky region, having previously included its whiskies in the Highland category for a number of years.

ISLAY

If Campbeltown was formerly Scotland's 'whisky capital', then Islay is most certainly the country's 'whisky island.' It is home to eight working distilleries, the most recently established being Kilchoman, a 'boutique,' farm-based operation which commenced production in 2005.

Once principally used for blending purposes, Islay single malts have become extremely fashionable during

the past couple of decades, with Ardbeg, Bowmore, Lagavulin and Laphroaig all gaining something approaching cult status with drinkers. One of the great success stories of Islay has been the re-opening of Bruichladdich distillery (see p.66).

Islays are generally regarded as the most assertive and distinctive of all Scotch malt whiskies, noted for their peaty and medicinal character, though there are great stylistic differences between the Kildalton distilleries of the southern Islay shore (Ardbeg, Laphroaig and Lagavulin) and the gentler, less dominant malts from further north on the island, including the gentle and very lightly peated Bunnahabhain.

ISLANDS

The Islands category of malt whiskies includes Scapa and the world-renowned Highland Park from the Orkney islands to the north of mainland Scotland, along with western distilleries such as Jura, Tobermory, and Arran. It also includes the mighty, complex and peppery Talisker from the Isle of Skye. This is a very disparate category of whiskies with the elegant and quite delicate Arran malt having little in common with Talisker, for example.

LOWLAND

The Lowland region of malt whisky production lies south of the theoretical line between Greenock and Dundee, which separates the Highlands from the Lowlands.

History has not been kind to the area, and today only Auchentoshan, near Glasgow, Bladnoch in the far west of Galloway, and Glenkinchie, south of Edinburgh, survive, along with a small-scale, farm-based distillery at Daft Mill in Fife, which gave new impetus to the classification when it opened during 2005.

Many connoisseurs consider Rosebank, near Falkirk, to have been the best Lowland of all. Sadly, however, it was the victim of a major 1980s rationalisation programme by owners The Distillers Company Ltd, and is now a lost distillery.

Stylistically, Lowlands tend to be comparatively light-bodied, aperitif whiskies, noted for their delicacy and soft, grassy aromas and flavours.

IRISH WHISKEY

Irish whiskey has a long and honourable heritage, and may even predate Scotch. The origins of both are lost in the mists of time (see p7). Most Irish whiskey differs from its Scottish counterpart not only in terms of spelling but also in ingredients and production methods (see p7).

Although there were 28 legal distilleries in production in Ireland in the late 19th century, that number has now fallen to three, one in Northern Ireland and two in the Republic. However, between them these three distilleries produce around 30 different whiskies. In general terms, Irish whiskies tend to be lighter in body and smoother than their Scottish counterparts.

BUSHMILLS

Bushmills distillery is located on the County Antrim coast near the Giant's Causeway in Northern Ireland. It was formally licensed in 1784, though successive owners have long claimed that its heritage actually dates back to 1608, when a licence was granted to distil in the area. Even today, bottles carry the legend 'The world's oldest whiskey distillery.' In 2005, Bushmills was purchased by drinks industry leader Diageo, having previously belonged to Pernod Ricard, owners of the Irish Distillers Company (see *Midleton,* p.41).

Bushmills triple distils malt whiskey, and while most still finds its way into blends such as Bushmills Irish Whiskey and Black Bush, quantities have been bottled as single malt since 1987, and these expressions have become increasingly popular in recent years.

COOLEY

Situated near Dundalk, just south of the Irish border, on the east coast, Cooley is a comparative newcomer to the Irish distilling scene. Cooley started life as an industrial alcohol plant, but was acquired in 1987 by Irish entrepreneur John Teeling, who added a pair of pot stills to the existing column still and took on the Irish Distillers Company's whiskey-making monopoly.

Cooley produces a number of blended whiskeys, a single grain whiskey and a single malt, named Tyrconnell, while the distillery's most idiosyncratic and interesting product is a peated single malt called Connemara. Tealing's company also owns the former Locke's distillery in Kilbeggan, which dates from 1757 and is now used solely to mature the Cooley spirit (see p18).

MIDLETON

Located 15 miles from Cork city, whiskey-making began at Midleton during the 1820s, and the original distillery now provides a range of visitor facilities. Its replacement dates from 1975, and is a complex, versatile plant which features six column stills and four pot stills, capable of providing many different spirit permutations.

Within Midleton, a wide range of whiskeys is produced, including the bestselling Irish blends Jameson's and Power's Gold Label, both formerly distilled in Dublin, along with the Cork favourite, Paddy.

AMERICAN WHISKEY

The classic American style of whiskeys are Bourbon and rye (see p27-8), though the latter is only now starting to find favour again after many decades of neglect. Before Bourbon came to prominence, rye was the principal style of whiskey consumed in America. The best ryes are as characterful, flavoursome and complex as a classic Scotch single malt, and leading rye whiskeys worth looking out for include Rittenhouse and Pikesville from Heaven Hill distillers and Sazerac and Van Winkle from Buffalo Trace.

Also something of a niche product, but an expanding one, is small batch Bourbon. Following the success of Scotch single malt whiskies, a number of American distillers have developed the concept of small-batch Bourbon, namely carefully chosen, premium bottlings of their finest

whiskeys. Seek out Knob Creek, Booker's Bourbon, Baker's and Wild Turkey Rare Breed.

Micro-distilling takes place in California, Oregon and West Virginia, while Virginia also boasts one full-scale distillery in the shape of the A Smith Bowman plant at Fredericksburg. However, the states of Kentucky and Tennessee are the heartland of US whiskey production, and home to such great names as Jim Beam, Maker's Mark, Wild Turkey and Jack Daniels.

KENTUCKY

Kentucky boasts 10 working distilleries, with Barton being located in the Bourbon 'capital' of Bardstown in Nelson County, once home to more than 20 distilleries. Wild Turkey and Four Roses distilleries are situated close to Lawrenceburg in Anderson County. Stylistically, Wild Turkey produces much heavier and more fully-flavoured whiskeys than its neighbour.

Kentucky's largest city of Louisville once boasted a dozen distilleries, but today houses just two, namely Brown-Forman and Bernheim. Brown-Forman produces the Early Times and Old Forester brands, while Bernheim distillery makes the Heaven Hill range, which features big bodied, sweet and spicy whiskeys of greater maturity. Heaven Hill is the largest independent, family-owned distilling company in the USA.

The other working Kentucky distilleries include Woodford

Reserve, which triple distils its spirit in Scottish-built pot stills and Maker's Mark, with its distinctive, red-sealed bottles and labels bearing the Scottish spelling of 'whisky.' Buffalo Trace distillery is situated at Frankfort, and specialises in producing characterful single barrel, rye, and wheated Bourbon whiskeys, while the world's best-selling Bourbon is Jim Beam, distilled at Clermont in Nelson County.

TENNESSEE

Tennessee whiskeys differ from Bourbon due to the distinctive charcoal filtration process which they undergo (see p27), and the state boasts two mainstream distil-leries in the shape of George A Dickel & Co's plant at Tullahoma in Coffee County and its much larger neigh-bour Jack Daniel's, situated less than 10 miles away at Lynchburg, in Nelson County.

Dickel whiskeys are lighter in style, sweet, aromatic and with distinctive vanilla notes, while Jack Daniel's whiskeys tend to be slightly more full-bodied and oilier.

Ironically, both are produced in essentially 'dry' counties, and though Jack Daniel's plays up its 'country-boy' roots and enduring folksy image, the distillery is owned by the large Brown-Forman organisation, whose product range also includes Southern Comfort, while George Dickel belongs to Diageo, the world's biggest drinks company.

Jack Daniel's has achieved what most other whiskey marketing departments can only dream of: namely making whiskey a 'cool' drink for young people. This is principally due to its association with rock stars such as Keith Richards of the Rolling Stones, and at a time when white spirits rule with the under 30s, 'JD and coke' is a notably popular exception to the rule in many clubs and bars.

CANADA

The vast country of Canada boasts almost the same number of distilleries as Kentucky, yet when did you last see any Canadian whisky in a bar, with the exception of the ubiquitous Canadian Club? Kentucky Bourbons are renowned – and available – the world over, but Canadians have a much lower international profile. Canadian distillers choose to use the Scottish spelling 'whisky' for their product rather than the more usual North American version of 'whiskey.'

Stylistically, Canadian whiskies tend to be blended ryes, light, fruity and comparatively sweet, and the great names of Canadian distilling include the now defunct Seagram company, once the world's foremost drinks producer.

Today, five distilleries operate in the prairie land of the Canadian west, along with three in Ontario and one in Quebec, while the most quirky is Glenora, located on Cape Breton island in Nova Scotia. Glenora was established in 1989 and produces pot still single malt whisky in traditional Scottish style.

JAPAN

The Japanese have long been adept at taking and developing existing concepts and products, usually improving them in the process. The inspiration for Japanese whisky distillation is Scottish, and stylistically most Japanese whiskies, malt and blended, bear a marked resemblance to those of Scotland.

The oldest working distillery in Japan is Yamazaki, founded in 1923 by Suntory, now one of the largest drinks companies in the world and owners of such iconic distilleries as Bowmore on the Hebridean island of Islay. As well as Yamazaki, Suntory boasts Hakushu distillery, the largest malt distillery in the world. Both operate Scottish-style pot stills. Having been in the business of selling blended whisky for many years, Suntory now produces a number of fine single malts, including 12-year-old expressions of Yamazaki and Hakushu.

Not to be outdone, Suntory's chief rival, Nikka, markets single malts and a range of popular blends, produced in its Yoichi and Sendai distilleries, the latter being equipped with both pot and column stills.

In addition to the 'big two', Fuji-Gotemba distillery is owned by Kirin Brewery Company Ltd, while Mercian operates the Karuizawa distillery. Both produce single malt whiskies, in addition to a selection of blends.

Overall, Japanese single malts can undoubtedly give the Scots a run for their money in terms of quality and character.

THE REST OF THE WORLD

In Europe, whisky is made in Austria, Belgium, France, Finland, Germany, Poland Switzerland, Sweden and Wales, where the Welsh Whisky Company Ltd has been distilling a single malt under the brand name of Penderyn since 2000. In England, distilleries are under construction at Staveley in the Lake District and near Thetford in Norfolk at the time of writing.

Further afield, India has a vast internal market for whisky, and boasts some ten working distilleries, while neighbouring Pakistan has one whisky-making facility. Whisky is also distilled in Turkey, Thailand Taiwan and South Africa, not to mention New Zealand and Australia, where it is produced in Melbourne and on the island of Tasmania.

DRINKING WHISKY

"Ye may tak a man tae drink,
but ye canna mak him water it"

There is still an enduring school of thought that considers it unmanly or plain vulgar to drink whisky any way other than neat. "There are two things the Highlander likes naked, and one of them is whisky," as the old saying goes. This is, of course, nonsense. Anyone who really knows anything about the subject will point out that a modest amount of pure, still water, served at room temperature helps to tease out aromas and flavours that might otherwise remain hidden. Certainly, if you are drinking cask strength whisky and you don't dilute it, you won't experience very much at all except indigestion and a headache.

Apart from adding water, just how should one drink whisky? The short answer is any way you choose to. You paid for it, so you can take it how you wish. If ice and cranberry juice help you enjoy your 15-year-old single malt, then so be it. One of the principal growth markets for Scotch whisky is China, where a fashion has developed for drinking certain deluxe blended whiskies like Chivas Regal and Johnnie Walker Black Label with green tea.

However, most connoisseurs would consider an expensive malt whisky or small batch Bourbon to be spoilt by the addition of anything but water. As one veteran Scotch whisky distiller puts it, "We take great care to make the finest spirit possible, employing men with 20

and even 30 years of experience. We fill it into carefully chosen casks and monitor it for maybe two decades before considering it perfect for bottling. Then someone pulls off the cap, pours it into a big tumbler onto a mound of ice and all those delicate aromas and tastes we've worked so hard to present to you are killed stone dead!"

It is important to serve whisky in a sensible glass, and for purposes of evaluation and comparison a stemmed copita or other glass which tapers towards the top is ideal. This serves to hold in the aromas rather than allowing them to escape into the atmosphere, making it much easier to detect and analyse components by nose. When drinking for pleasure rather than professional reasons, a small tumbler is best, ideally something large enough to hold the whisky and water, but not so large that your dram gets lost in the bottom of it.

Professional tasters usually evaluate whisky using four factors: colour, nose, palate and finish.

The colour of a whisky may well give you clues to the type of cask in which it has been matured. If it is a deep, rich copper colour it has probably come from a European Oak cask, formerly used to hold sherry. A pale, straw-coloured whisky was probably matured in an American Oak cask that previously stored Bourbon. Look at the 'legs' of the whisky, as it rolls down the side of the glass. A well-aged, full-bodied whisky will have 'longer' legs than a younger, light-bodied example.

Nose is crucial to whisky analysis because while a human being has some 9,000 taste buds he or she has between 50 and 100 million olfactory receptors. Smell is undoubtedly the most important of our five senses when it comes to analysing whisky, and most blenders work almost entirely by nose.

A vocabulary of six broad terms has been developed to describe aromas; namely cereal, estery, floral, peaty, feinty, sulphury and woody. However, for the untrained nose, this part of the process is principally about evocation; for example, a smell that suddenly takes you back to a childhood day playing by a fishing harbour, recalling old fish boxes, tarry ropes and seaweed.

In terms of flavour and what may be termed 'mouth-feel,' professionals may use the adjectives sweet, sour, salty, bitter, warming, cooling, prickly, viscous and cloying. The 'finish' is the lingering flavour of the whisky in the mouth after swallowing has taken place. In general terms, a long finish is desirable, though some lighter-bodied whiskies benefit from a short, crisp finish.

Whenever tasting whiskies, beware the power of suggestion! If undertaking an informal tasting session with friends, it is advisable to ask each sampler to write down his or her reactions before discussing them. Otherwise, if someone informs the group during tasting that the nose of a particular whisky reminds him or her of the leather upholstery of a pre-war Daimler, sure enough, everyone else will immediately detect the same smell.

A few basic rules to remember: Don't wear strong perfume or after-shave lotion while tasting, otherwise even the most pungent Islay may have a nose like Chanel. The same applies to eating garlic and chilli sauce just before sampling whisky.

When diluting whisky, try to be consistent, and always dilute to the same degree. Comparisons are much more accurate that way. In practice, younger and lighter-bodied whiskies will stand up to less dilution than old and big-bodied spirits.

It may pay to take a small, preliminary sip after nosing the whisky undiluted, in order to give a 'baseline,' then add just a few drops of water before nosing it again. Follow up with a second, comparative sip.

It is also interesting to leave the whisky to stand for a few moments after your initial nosing. Sometimes you will be surprised at just how much it changes after exposure to the air.

Our noses and palates tend to be at their keenest earlier in the day, and it is instructive to experiment with whiskies at different times. Mid-morning, a light, delicate Lowland or Speyside whisky might seem to have lots of character, but sampled late in the evening, after a meal and perhaps a glass of wine, it could seem singularly bland. By the same token, an assertive Islay which is perfect as an after dinner fireside dram might well overwhelm before lunch.

And the most important point of all. The whole process should be about enjoyment and fruitful experimentation. Have fun!

On the subject of fruitful experimentation, here are some whisky-based cocktails that you may wish to try:

Hot Irish
Not strictly a cocktail, more of a punch, but an ideal whiskey drink for outdoor events in winter. Stud a lemon segment with four cloves, then pour a measure of Irish whiskey into a stemmed glass. Add two teaspoons of brown sugar and the lemon. Fill with boiling water and add a pinch of cinnamon.

Hot Toddy
A hot toddy usually consists of Scotch whisky, lemon juice and honey, though some drinkers dismiss honey and advocate dissolving three or four lumps of sugar in a tumbler of boiling water, then adding the whisky. Purists frown on the inclusion of lemon juice. Ideally, the whisky should be a malt, as blended whiskies tend to give off rather unpleasant fumes when added to hot water.

Manhattan
A truly classic cocktail, with its origins in New York, a recipe for the Manhattan first appeared in Harry Johnson's 1882 *Bartenders' Manual*. Take one measure of

rye whiskey or Bourbon, half a measure of dry vermouth, half a measure of sweet vermouth and a dash of angustora bitters. Stir, strain into a cocktail glass and serve with a cocktail cherry.

Mint Julep
A signature whiskey drink of the American south. Muddle four fresh mint sprigs with a teaspoon of sugar and either a little soda or water in a tall glass, then add crushed ice and at least two ounces of Bourbon. Garnish with mint.

Old-Fashioned
Traditionalists specify rye whiskey as the base for an old-fashioned, though many drinkers now favour Bourbon or even Scotch whisky. Muddle one teaspoon of sugar, six dashes of angustora bitters, a dash of soda, one slice of orange and one cherry in an old-fashioned cocktail glass. Remove the orange rind, add two ounces of whiskey, ice and another dash of soda. Garnish with a cherry and a second slice of orange.

Rusty Nail
Take one and a half ounces of whisky, ideally single malt Scotch, plus half an ounce of Drambuie, Glayva or Loch Fyne Scotch Whisky Liqueur. Mix and serve over ice.

Whisky Mac
Mix one and a half ounces of whisky and one ounce of green ginger wine. A great winter warmer.

Whisky Sour
Shake together one and a half ounces of whisky, the juice of half a lemon and half a teaspoon of sugar. Serve over ice and with a dash of soda water in an old-fashioned cocktail glass. Bourbon or rye may be substituted for Scotch, giving a Whiskey Sour.

WHISKY TALES

—— SCOTCH DRINK ——

O thou, my Muse! Guid auld Scotch drink,
Whether through wimplin' worms thou jink,
Or, richly brown, ream o'er the brink,
In glorious faem,
Inspire me, till I lisp and wink,
To sing thy name!

Robert Burns – *Scotch Drink* (1785).

Scotland's greatest poet - and most passionate advocate of whisky – also served as an excise officer, being based in Dumfries from 1789 until his untimely death in 1796. As well as writing several fine poems on the subject of whisky, he penned the tongue-in-cheek song *The Deil's Awa'Wi'The Exciseman* in 1792, reputedly while hiding in a salt marsh on the Solway Firth, keeping a boat suspected of smuggling under surveillance.

—— SINISTER SPIRITS ——

Glenrothes distillery, in the Speyside town of Rothes, is located alongside the local cemetery, allowing ample scope for word play about 'spirits', and The Glenrothes does indeed feature a ghost story in its rich heritage.

This tale concerns African born Biawa Makalanga, brought to Rothes in 1898 by Major James Grant of Glen Grant distillery. The Major had found him as an abandoned child during a hunting expedition in Matabeleland. Biawa worked as the Grants' butler until the Major's death in 1931, after which he lived on in Glen Grant House until his own death in 1972.

Some eight years later, soon after a new, greatly enlarged Glenrothes stillhouse had been built, the apparition of Biawa began to appear to distillery workers. Biawa's presence seems to have been entirely benign, but was enough for the Glenrothes management to bring in the celebrated psychic investigator Professor Cedric Wilson.

He deduced that a ley-line had been disturbed by the new construction, and after instructing that a stake of pig iron should be erected on either side of the still house, he proceeded to walk without hesitation to a grave in the nearby cemetery, which he had never previously visited. According to distillery staff, observing from a discreet distance, he talked for some minutes before returning to the distillery, declaring that the matter had been amicably resolved. The grave belonged to Biawa Makalanga.

No further sightings of Biawa occurred. As Glenrothes' longest serving member of staff Roger Johnston puts it, "In the 33 years here, I have seen plenty spirits, but none that walk!"

Meanwhile, up at Glenmorangie distillery at Tain on the Scottish east coast, a ghost known as the White Lady was said to haunt the maltings, and the very sight of her could drive a man mad. In the days when malt was turned by hand on distillery malting floors, it often fell to the apprentices to complete this back-breaking chore, and the warmth of the atmosphere and the toil of the job meant that it would be very easy to fall asleep in the middle of a shift, potentially ruining the 'piece' of unturned malt. On their first day at work, successive Glenmorangie distillery managers would warn new apprentices about the White Lady. Curiously, none of them ever fell asleep in the maltings!

The former Scotch whisky 'capital' of Campbeltown in Argyllshire also had its share of ghosts, including one resident at Glen Scotia distillery. Glen Scotia was owned by one Duncan MacCallum from 1924 to 1928, when it fell silent, and the story goes that MacCallum was defrauded of the enormous sum of £40,000 by a group of con men. In his distress he drowned himself in Cross Hill Loch, from which the distillery takes its process water. However, another version of the story says that he hanged himself in the distillery mill room. Apparently, one stillman subsequently hated going up to the mill room alone at night because he regularly sensed an eerie presence there.

IRISH COFFEE

Irish or Gaelic coffee has served to raise the profile of Irish whiskey in recent years. Actually a variation on the traditional Irish drink of sweet tea with whiskey, it usually consists of coffee, sugar, whiskey and cream. The drink was invented in 1952 at Shannon airport in the west of Ireland by chef Joe Sheridan, who served it one cold evening to an American journalist. The journalist introduced it to the 'Buena Vista' on Fisherman's Wharf, overlooking San Francisco Bay, and Irish Coffee was rapidly embraced across the USA and far beyond.

A TOUCH TOO MUCH

We have all, at times, got carried away and partaken of just a little too much of our favourite tipple. One of Scotland's most popular hangover cures is a bottle of the country's 'other' national drink, Irn Bru. The Japanese apparently eat a pickled cherry the morning after a bout of over-indulgence, while a voodoo cure from Haiti involves sticking 13 pins into the cork from the bottle that caused the trouble in the first place. More conventional is the Cognac-based Prairie Oyster, while the earliest recorded hangover cure dates from 479BC, and is the work of the Greek philosopher Antiphanes:

> "Take the hair, it is well written
> of the dog by which you are bitten
> work off one wine by his brother
> one labour with another."

US actor and humorist WC Fields was an enthusiastic drinker, particularly of whiskey, and his favoured hangover cure was a martini, consisting of one part vermouth and four parts gin, not to mention an olive.

"Always carry a flagon of whiskey in case of a snake bite," Fields advised. "And furthermore, always carry a small snake."

Legendary 'Rat Pack' crooner and serious imbiber Dean Martin had a simple way of avoiding a hangover. "Stay drunk."

THE KING OF DRINKS

In August 1822 King George IV made a state visit to Scotland, and this momentous occasion was largely stage-managed by the poet and novelist Sir Walter Scott, who created a *Brigadoon*-style extravaganza of kitsch Scottishness for the monarch.

In his 1848 *Life of Sir Walter Scott*, JG Lockhart wrote of the king's arrival in the port of Leith. "…On receiving the poet on the quarter-deck, his Majesty called for a bottle of Highland whisky, and having drunk his health in this national liquor, desired a glass to be filled for him. Sir Walter, after draining his own bumper, made a request that the King would condescend to bestow on him the glass out of which His Majesty had just drunk his health; and this being granted, the precious vessel was immediately wrapped up and carefully deposited in what he conceived to be the safest part of his dress."

Unfortunately, when he returned home, Scott managed to sit on the glass, shattering his precious royal souvenir to pieces.

Lockhart refers to "Highland whisky," but we can be more specific, as Elizabeth Grant of Rothiemurchus wrote of the occasion in her *Memoirs of A Highland Lady* (1898) "Lord Conyngham, the Chamberlain, was looking everywhere for pure Glenlivet whisky: the king drank nothing else."

At that time, the Glenlivet area in north-east Scotland was a hotbed of illicit distillation. The king's favourite whisky was, then, almost certainly illicitly distilled, though George Smith 'went legit' in 1824, much to the fury of his fellow former illicit distillers, who threatened to burn his new Glenlivet distillery to the ground.

Clearly the monarch was a man of some taste in matters alcoholic, since Glenlivet was synonymous with the highest quality whisky, even if it was distilled without benefit of licence. As the legal distilling trade grew during the later 19th century, so many north-east distilleries added the 'Glenlivet' suffix to their names in order to cash in on its reputation that it was dubbed 'the longest glen in Scotland.'

─────── WOMBYLING FREE ───────

Writing of whisky in his *Chronicles of England, Scotland and Ireland* (1577) Raphael Holinshed observed that "Being moderately taken it cutteth fleume, it lighteneth the mynd, it quickeneth the spirits, it cureth the hydropsie, it pounceth the stone, it repelleth gravel, it puffeth away ventositie, it kepyth and preserveth the eyes from dazelying, the tongue from lispying, the teeth from chatterying, the throte from rattlying, the weasan from stieflying, the stomach from womblying, e harte from swellying, the bellie from wirtching, the guts from rumblying, the hands from shivering, the sinews from shrinkying, the veynes from crumplying, the bones from akying, the marrow from soakying, and truly it is a sovereign liquor if it be orderlie taken".

Now there's an endorsement!

─── MAKING A SCOTSMAN HAPPY ───

In his 1775 publication *A Journey to the Western Isles of Scotland*, Dr Samuel Johnson wrote "They are not a drunken race but no man is so abstemious as to refuse the morning dram, which they call a skalk."

Johnson's companion on that expedition to the Hebrides was his friend and biographer James Boswell, who recalled in his own account of their travels (published in 1784) the first time Johnson tasted whisky, while staying at an Inveraray inn.

"We supped well; and after supper, Dr. Johnson, whom I had not seen taste any fermented liquor during all our travels, called for a gill of whisky.

'Come (said he) let me know what it is that makes a Scotchman happy!'

He drank it all but a drop, which I begged him leave

to pour into a glass that I might say we had drunk whisky together."

CIVIL DRINKING

During the American Civil War (1861-1865) both Union and Confederate generals drank whiskey on a daily basis, though Confederate general Robert E Lee once declared "I like it: I always did, and that is the reason I never use it." Whiskey served both to raise morale among the troops and also as an anaesthetic when limbs had to be amputated. US president Abraham Lincoln famously said of his bibulous yet strategically brilliant general (and subsequent president) Ulysses S Grant, "Let me know what brand of whiskey Grant uses. For if it makes fighting generals like Grant, I should like to get some of it for distribution."

WHISKY GALORE

Whisky Galore is undoubtedly the most famous film relating to Scotch whisky, and the 1949 Ealing Comedy was based on Compton Mackenzie's best-selling novel, published two years previously. The fictional events of the film and novel had their origins in the wrecking of the *SS Politician* off the Hebridean island of Eriskay in February 1941. Part of its cargo was 24,000 tonnes of spirits, principally whisky, and the thirsty, war-weary islanders set about looting it with great enthusiasm. It has been estimated that around 2,000 cases (or a highly impressive 24,000 bottles) were 'liberated' from the vessel. Several islanders who were caught in the act of looting received fines of between £10 and £30, though several were also sent to prison for two months. Of the 24,000 bottles reportedly removed from the 'Polly,' few survive today. In

November 1987, eight bottles were auctioned in Edinburgh and fetched a total of £4,000. Such is the enduring fascination with the *Whisky Galore* legend that in January 2003 a mere wooden panel from one of the cases of 'Polly' whisky sold at Bonham's auction house in London for a sum in excess of £1,500.

LIES, DAMNED LIES AND STATISTICS

Scotch whisky is truly a drink for the world, and in 2005 exports increased by four per cent to a grand total of £2.36 billion, with almost 990 million bottles being sold worldwide. Consequently, this was the third best year for exports in the history of Scotch, and sales of malt whisky rose by eight per cent to their highest ever level.

China continues to be *the* boom market, with exports up by no less than 86 per cent, while overall in Asia they increased by 24 per cent. India also has the potential to be a massive market for Scotch. However, high discriminatory tariffs which favour locally-distilled spirit at the expense of imported whiskies will have to be overcome before a breakthrough is reached there. Russia, too, is developing a taste for Scotch whisky, particularly malts.

Here in the UK, though, sales of Scotch actually fell by six per cent. The message is clear: we need to drink more. Though obviously we also need to drink responsibly!

WHISKY TASTING RECORDS

In July 2005 the Easy Drinking Whisky Company claimed a place in the *Guinness Book of Records* for the 'world's largest whisky tasting,' after 1,661 people sampled all three of the firm's whiskies at the Royal Highland Show in Edinburgh. The record had previously been held by a Stockholm whisky festival, staged in November 2001, which involved 1,210 tasters.

The Swedes were not prepared to take the loss of their status lying down, however, and responded by insisting that their record was for 'batch tasting,' with each of the 1,210 drinkers sampling six different whiskies in a formal tasting scenario, and therefore consuming far more whisky in total than at the Scottish event.

Does it matter? Not really. But, for the record the previous largest 'batch tasting' prior to the Stockholm triumph took place in Japan, where a mere 520 persons participated. It seems likely, however, that the record for whisky consumed had already been broken at a number of whisky festivals when no one was counting, and, for that matter, on Friday evenings in the bars and clubs of Glasgow, Tokyo and Dufftown...

WHISKY ROLLERS

Two tales from someone closely connected with a Speyside whisky company. The teller wishes to remain anonymous...

"Willie Phillips was managing director of Macallan-Glenlivet, as the company was latterly called when it was still independent. He had a Rolls Royce, and one evening Willie was driving home when he saw a member of the Macallan staff and his bicycle lying in a ditch close to the distillery entrance. Willie got out of his Rolls and approached the man, asking if he could be of any assistance.

'Well,' replied the worker, who had presumably found his way into a cask in one of the warehouses, 'I was just thinking, it's a strange thing whisky. It puts you up there in a Rolls Royce and me down here in a ditch.'

Some folk will do anything for a free dram, even if

getting caught means getting fired. Back in the early 1970s I was working in the shipping department of the old Black & White whisky bottling operation at Stepps in Glasgow. At one time stuff was going missing from the bottling line, and they had two female security staff who randomly searched lots of the women who worked on the line, and despite all their efforts they found nothing. Finally, management thought 'what is the common denominator here?' Headscarves. So they got one woman to take off her headscarf, and under it she had those big plastic hair rollers that they wore in the '70s. And pushed into each one was a miniature bottle of Black & White whisky! They'd all been doing it for weeks...

Mind you, at the same time just about everyone in the shipping department was sitting at their desk with a bottle of Irn Bru in front of them, which they swigged from all day. The only thing was, it was three-quarters whisky and one-quarter Irn Bru. The department manager knew all about this, because he had a bottle too..."

CATNIP

One of the more bizarre records in the Scotch whisky industry belongs to Towser, the late, lamented Glenturret distillery cat, who earned herself a place in the *Guinness Book of Records* by dispatching no fewer than 28,899 mice during her 24 years at the Perthshire distillery. The tortoiseshell terror is now immortalised in a statue close to the Glenturret visitor centre, which also serves as home to the Famous Grouse Experience.

Towser's successor, Amber, proved less of a dedicated huntress, and was never known to catch a mouse at all, but, in 2005, after an extensive trawl of Scotland's Cat Protection shelters, not one but two replacement felines were found. One was the ginger and white 'gentle giant' Dylan, from Forfar, and the other was the semi-long haired Glaswegian female Brooke.

The Famous Grouse PR team did a fine job in getting a disproportionate amount of exposure for the story in all sections of the media, and the Aberdeen-based *Press & Journal* even printed photographs of all nine short-listed feline hopefuls!

Grouse PR Manager Carol McLaren said "We are delighted to finally have not one but two cats in position at the distillery and we are sure the charismatic Dylan and beautiful Brooke will soon be firm favourites."

She added "Dylan has already thrown himself into the spirit of things…"

Not literally, we hope.

Meanwhile, two centuries of tradition at Highland Park on Orkney were broken with the death of Barley, the distillery cat, in March 2006, when it was decided by bosses not to find a replacement. Barley, a 15-year-old ginger tom, was a great favourite with locals and tourists and received many Christmas presents and cards.

Jason Craig, global controller for Highland Park, said "Barley was a real character and there are many tales surrounding his time at the distillery. He was very friendly to tourists, but this warmth did not extend to dogs - he was renowned for terrorising the former distillery manager's hound, which once had to be carried from the distillery as he was too frightened to move. His favourite spot was, unbelievably, on top of the money till in the Highland Park shop, and many tourists thought he was a toy, so they got quite a shock when they touched him on the back."

Barley was the last of a group of three kittens raised as distillery cats at Highland Park, and his siblings were named Malt and Peat by distillery workers.

"We are considering a number of suggestions as to how we could commemorate the cats, which would also act as a mark of respect," said Craig. "One suggestion is to commission a local artist to make a statue which will be displayed in the courtyard, as they will always be part of the distillery's heritage. We have decided not to replace

Barley due to environmental regulations, though we are sure he will be sadly missed by visitors. The decision was not taken lightly."

As though Towser's record was not strange enough, back in the 1970s, Cutty Sark whisky offered a £1 million prize to anyone who could capture the Loch Ness Monster alive. Dead, presumably, would have been bad for the drink's image.

The canny company insured itself against the possibility of having to pay out the prize money, and the policy stipulated that the monster, if caught, should be taken to London and identified as 'Nessie' by a professional zoologist.

WHISKY AS A WEAPON OF MASS DESTRUCTION

It has long been conceded by industry rivals that when it comes to generating column inches in newspapers and magazines and gaining general exposure, the boys at Bruichladdich distillery on Islay punch way above their weight.

Bruichladdich is the classic story of a distillery abandoned by its global owners and rescued from oblivion and mothballs by a small team of dedicated specialists, led by London wine merchant Mark Reynier and Islay distilling legend Jim McEwan. Having closed in 1994, production recommenced at Bruichladdich in May 2001, and the Bruichladdich website boasts that the distillery is run by people using Victorian equipment rather than by computers.

As a small team of niche players, Reynier and co have become adept at undertaking newsworthy developments, and fitted out Bruichladdich distillery with webcams so that members of the public could feel an involvement with all the processes of whisky-making.

This led to the bizarre situation in 2003 when it was revealed that the American Defence Threat Reduction Agency had been monitoring the distillery via its webcams, as the distilling process seemed to them to be suspiciously similar to that used to create weapons of mass destruction.

Destruction – this time of the liver – seems a distinct possibility with a 2006 Bruichladdich development, as the Islay innovators recreated an ancient and highly potent triple-distilled spirit, inspired by the writings of legendary traveller Martin Martin, who described sampling a similar spirit during a visit to Islay back in 1695.

Instead of peaking at around 65 per cent, as the strongest Scotch whiskies currently do, Trestarig (pronounced *trace-arak*) was casked at 84.5 per cent. As the Bruichladdich folk say, "At that strength it will protect you from anything."

WASHINGTON'S STILL

The first president of the United States, George Washington, was also a distiller, who built a large-scale distillery on his Mount Vernon estate in Virginia in 1797. As an army general, Washington had advocated the supply of spirits to his troops to combat the effects of fatigue and inhospitable weather. "The benefits arising from the moderate use of strong liquor have been experienced in all armies and are not to be disputed," he wrote.

In 1939 a still believed to have come from Washington's original distillery was captured by revenue officers. It bore the legend 'Made in Bristol, England, 1783.' The still was discovered during a raid on an illicit whiskey-making operation run by a black family who were direct descendents of slaves on Washington's Mount Vernon estate.

In 2000 excavation and restoration work began on Washington's distillery, and 18th century-style stills were subsequently installed in the reconstructed buildings. The site opened to the public in 2007, and is the only operating 18th century-style distillery in North America. It functions as a national distilling museum and the gateway to the American Whiskey Trail, which encompasses historic distilling-related sites in New York, Pennsylvania, Virginia, Kentucky and Tennessee.

————————WHISKY BANGALORE ————

Until recently, very few British drinkers could claim to have tasted Indian whisky, but the arrival of Amrut on UK shores has changed all that. Amrut takes its name from the nectar drunk by the Hindu Gods, and is made using Indian malted barley grown in the north-west Indian frontier states of Rajasthan and Punjab. This is malted in Delhi and Jaipur, before the actual distilling process takes place in Amrut Distilleries Ltd's plant in the southern city of Bangalore.

Bangalore is situated some 3,000 feet above sea level, and Amrut is matured in what can only be described as 'tropical' conditions on the distillery site. Not surprisingly, given India's climate, maturation is intense, with a notable high 'angels' share' of up to 15 per cent bulk lost through evaporation each year. In these conditions, three years in imported oak casks is enough to fully mature the spirit, and anyone expecting Amrut to be 'firewater' is in for a pleasant surprise.

Amrut Single Malt may be a new kid on the whisky block, having been launched in Glasgow in 2004, but Amrut Distilleries Ltd was founded back in 1948 by Radhakrishna Jagdale. It was Rakshit 'Ricky' Jagdale, grandson of the company founder, who developed the radical plan to market Amrut as a single malt in the UK while studying for an MBA at the University of Newcastle upon Tyne.

Inevitably, the press had a field day with 'coals to Newcastle-style' stories about Amrut's Scottish debut, but Jagdale says "We wanted to launch our product in the home of all malts. We felt that if are able to launch successfully in Scotland, we can meet the criteria for the world market."

WHISKY CHASERS

The connection between horse racing and whisky may seem tenuous, with the obvious exceptions of drinking it while backing losers, or the sponsorship opportunities it affords, but this is not always the case. The County Cork racehorse trainer Fergie Sutherland regularly applied *poitín* to the legs of his 1986 Cheltenham Gold Cup winner Imperial Call after exercise, echoing an age-old tradition believed to have begun with early Christian monks in Egypt, who rubbed alcohol into the stiff legs of their mules.

More recently, after winning the prestigious King's Stand Stakes at Royal Ascot in June 2006 with his horse Takeover Target, Australian trainer Joe Janiak announced that he would probably spend the evening "having a few drinks with the horse." He went on to explain that the seven-year-old sprinter enjoyed a few 'tinnies' of lager after a big race, adding "and he occasionally has a Bourbon on the rocks, too!"

"Happiness is having a rare steak,
a bottle of whiskey, and a dog to eat the rare steak"
Johnny Carson

WHISKY CHARACTERS

The whisky industry has long boasted more than its fair share of colourful characters, and here we celebrate some of the key figures in the development of our great drink.

JOHNNIE WALKER

With its iconic 'striding man' image, Johnnie Walker is one of the world's best known and best selling Scotch whiskies. Like many others, this internationally renowned brand had its origins in humble circumstances. Ayrshire farmer's son John Walker invested in a grocery and wines and spirits business in Kilmarnock in 1820, but his serious involvement with whisky really began during the 1850s, when his son, Alexander, began blending whiskies and persuaded his father to concentrate on wholesaling rather than retailing the spirit. When Alexander took control of the firm on his father's death in 1857 whisky sales represented just eight per cent of the firm's income, but by the time Alexander handed the business over to his sons, whisky accounted for more than 90 per cent of turnover. Indeed, by the 1880s, John Walker & Sons Ltd was one of Scotland's largest blending companies, expanding into distilling with the purchase of Cardhu distillery in 1893. John Walker lives on in the 'striding man' logo, a depiction of him sketched by Tom Brown in 1908 and most recently seen adorning the air intakes of

Maclaren Formula One racing cars as part of a multi-million pound sponsorship deal.

AENEAS COFFEY

Although the Scottish distiller Robert Stein pioneered continuous distillation, it was Dublin born Aeneas Coffey who perfected the process, patenting his still in 1830. This invention paved the way for the hugely important development of blended whisky later in the century. Coffey was born in 1780, and worked as an excise officer for 25 years, enjoying a distinguished career and receiving bayonet wounds in an encounter with illicit distillers. Eventually he rose to the rank of Inspector General of Excise for Ireland before resigning from the service and buying the Dock distillery in his native city. It was there that much of the work was done to create his 'patent' still, and in 1838 he established Coffey & Son to manufacture patent stills. Ironically, Coffey's revolutionary still inflicted a great deal of harm on the Irish whiskey industry, as Irish distillers stubbornly stuck to their pot stills, while during the late 19th and early 20th centuries Scottish distillers proceeded to oust Irish spirit from its British strongholds with their blended whisky.

WILLIAM GRANT

Born in Dufftown in 1839, William Grant learnt his whisky-making trade in the town's Mortlach distillery, where he rose from the position of book-keeper to become manager. Grant was keen to develop his own distilling operation, however, and during 1886/87 worked with his family to build Glenfiddich, hiring only one mason and a carpenter to provide skilled labour. Grant had nine children, most of whom contributed to the financing, creation and running of the distillery, with son

Alec acting as stillman, Charlie as mashman and George as maltman. During quiet times, the Grant boys would study for university, and on one occasion when an excise supervisor named Burnet visited Glenfiddich, he came across a Latin grammar book lying open on a ledge in the malt barn. In another corner of the buildings he found a volume on mathematics, and in the stillhouse, a book of medical anatomy. Burnet declared that in all the many distilleries he had visited he'd never seen anything like it! The canny William Grant had been able to acquire second hand distilling plant from Cardhu for the bargain price of less than £120, and on Christmas Day 1887 the first spirit ran from the Glenfiddich stills. Today William Grant & Sons Ltd remains proudly independent, and is the fourth largest producer of Scotch whisky in the world.

JACK DANIEL

Jack Daniel was the youngest of ten children, born around 1846 in Tennessee, and at the age of seven he left home to live with an uncle, as he and his step-mother did not see eye to eye. He was soon helping local lay preacher and farmer Dan Call (himself just 17 years old) to make corn whiskey, being taught the art by Call's slave, Nearest Green. When Call decided to preach full time, he sold the whiskey business to 14-year-old Jack, who ultimately moved the business to its present location at Cave Spring Hollow, near Lynchburg. The diminutive Jack Daniel became a wealthy and highly eligible man, though he never married. Somewhat bizarrely, he died in 1911 from an injury caused when he stubbed a toe on a jammed safe door.

The distillery was silent during prohibition, but was subsequently re-opened by Jack Daniel's nephew, Lem Motlow, who left it to his sons on his death in 1947. The family sold it to Brown-Forman in 1956, and it remains in their hands today. The Lynchburg distillery is a place of pilgrimage for many whiskey lovers, who are able to buy any number of branded Jack Daniel souvenirs, but none of the actual product, as Moore County is still nominally 'dry.'

SAM BRONFMAN

The Bronfman family has had a greater influence on whisk(e)y in North America than any other. The Bronfmans originally left Russia to escape from the tsarist regime, and in 1924 Sam, aged 35, established the Distillers Corporation in Montreal. Prohibition helped to make the Bronfmans rich, with gangster Lucky Luciano declaring "Sam Bronfman was bootleggin' enough whiskey across the Canadian border to double the size of Lake Erie. It was no wonder that wags in the liquor trade were beginning to refer to Lake Erie as 'the Jewish lake.'"

The Bronfmans subsequently acquired the Seagram company, which eventually became the largest distiller in the world. Key to the growth of Seagram's was Sam Bronfman, who was determined to produce high quality whiskey in the post-Prohibition era. He was one of the great advocates of skilful blending, famously declaring "distilling is a science, but blending is an art." Under the control of 'Mr Sam,' Seagram also expanded into the UK market after the Second World War, initially purchasing the Chivas Regal brand and Strathisla distillery, and subsequently building a major power base on Speyside.

MASATAKA TAKETSURU

Masataka Taketsuru can be credited as the principal 'founding father' of the Japanese whisky industry. His family distilled sake, and the young Masataka spent two years in Scotland from 1918, studying chemistry at

Glasgow University. During this time, he worked for spells at Hazelburn distillery in Campbeltown and Longmorn, near Elgin, learning the secrets of Scotch whisky production and blending. While in Scotland he met and married doctor's daughter Jessie Roberta, known as Rita, who returned with him to Japan where she taught English. Taketsuru's knowledge of Scotch whisky distillation enabled the Suntory company to establish its first distillery at Yamazaki on the island of Honshu in 1923. Taketsuru subsequently left Suntory to set up Nikka Whisky in 1934, building a distillery in Yoichi on Japan's northern island of Hokkaido. His contribution to the creation and development of a viable Japanese whisky industry was immense.

TOMMY DEWAR

'Whisky Tom' Dewar was one of the foremost evangelists of the late 19th century blended whisky boom. Born in 1864, the flamboyant Tommy Dewar was one of the great characters of the industry, working with his lower profile brother, John, to establish Dewar's among the world's leading blended whiskies. Tommy Dewar famously arrived in London at the age of 21 with two business contacts, one of whom turned out to be bankrupt and the other dead. He was a difficult man to deter, however, and by the time the Perth-based firm of John Dewar & Sons Ltd merged with the Distillers Company Ltd in 1925, annual profits had risen from £1,321 in 1880 to £1,198,154. Noted for his 'Dewarisms,' such as "We have a great regard for old age when it is bottled," Tommy ended his days as one of the elite group of 'whisky barons,' which included his brother John and their great rival James Buchanan, creator of the 'Black & White' blend.

JOHN JAMESON

There are two varying versions of the John Jameson story. In one he is said to have been born into a Presbyterian family in the Scottish brewing centre of Alloa, and served as Sheriff of Clackmannanshire, being related through his wife to the powerful Haig and Stein distilling dynasties in central Scotland and Dublin. According to this story, he resigned from the post of sheriff and moved to Ireland, where he subsequently acquired the Bow Street distillery in Dublin. However, the alternative version of the story has John Jameson's father visiting Dublin in 1784, with John meeting and marrying Stein's daughter while staying in the city. Whichever account is true, Jameson is thought to have purchased the Bow Street distillery in 1805, naming the firm John Jameson & Son five years later. The old distillery now serves as a museum and visitor centre for Irish Distillers, and though distilled at Midleton in County Cork rather than in Dublin, Jameson's remains the world's best selling Irish whiskey.

MALCOLM GILLESPIE

In the heyday of illicit distillation in Scotland, excise officers or 'gaugers' faced danger on a regular basis while carrying out their duties. One of the highest profile gaugers was Malcolm Gillespie, who spent much of his career battling whisky smugglers in north-east Scotland. Gillespie trained a bull-terrier to seize smugglers' horses by their noses in order to make them rear up and drop their loads. This method proved highly successful, indeed too successful, since the dog was shot dead by a smuggler after just a few months of activity.

Gillespie was one of the most dedicated and industrious gaugers in Scotland, but his celebrity is due principally to the fact that he was one of the very few members of the excise service to be hanged. Gillespie's crime was the capital offence of forgery, for which he was executed in Aberdeen on 16th November 1827. In a statement made before his execution, Gillespie claimed to have in excess of 40 wounds on his body as a result of his work. During his 28 years with the excise service, he was responsible for the seizure of an astonishing 6,535 gallons of whisky, 62,400 gallons of wash, 407 stills, and even 85 carts and 165 horses!

GEORGE SMITH

George Smith founded the iconic Glenlivet distillery, the first to be licensed under the provisions of the 1823 Excise Act. Smith had previously supplemented his farming income by distilling on an illicit basis, and many of his fellow former 'smugglers' were less than pleased when Smith took the legal route, threatening to burn his new distillery at Upper Drumin to the ground. The Laird of Aberlour presented Smith with a pair of hair-trigger pistols, which the distiller carried for several years, even taking them to church with him and sleeping with them under his pillow.

As business boomed, Smith built a second distillery at Delnabo, near Tomintoul, but demand still outstripped supply. A larger distillery was subsequently constructed at Minmore in 1859, and The Glenlivet malt whisky continues to be made on that site. In seeing the advantages of distilling within the law, and working in a practical way to implement the Excise Act, Smith played a significant part in the development of the modern Scotch whisky industry we know today.

WHISKY WORDS

Angels' share – A distillers' term for *maturation* losses. In Scotland, some two per cent of all maturing whisky evaporates through the porous oak *casks* each year, but in hotter and more humid climates the losses may be much greater.

Blend – Many countries produce blended whiskies, using a variety of cereals, some malted and some unmalted, but a blended Scotch whisky is one made from a mixture of grain and malt spirit. Theoretically, the higher the malt content the better the blend, although this is not always the case. Much depends on the quality and age of grain and malt whiskies used.

Blended malt – Previously known in Scotland as 'vatted malt,' blended malt is a combination of two or more malt whiskies, and contains no grain spirit.

Brewing – The process which follows *malting* in the production of malt whisky, and consists of *mashing* and *fermentation*, though in Irish distilling circles it is usually taken to mean just mashing, with fermentation being considered a separate, successive operation.

Butt – The second largest size of cask regularly used by the whisky industry for maturation purposes. A butt contains approximately 110 gallons or 500 litres, twice the amount of a *hogshead*.

Cask – A generic term for containers of varying capacity in which spirit is stored during maturation.

Cask strength – Whisky sold at cask strength has not been diluted to the standard 40 per cent or 43 per cent, but is bottled at the strength at which it leaves the cask. This will vary depending on the age of the whisky, as older whiskies lose considerable strength during extended maturation.

Chill-filtering – The process of refrigerating whisky and finely filtering it to ensure it retains its clarity in the bottle and when water is added by the consumer. Many connoisseurs consider that chill-filtration detracts from the character of the whisky in subtle ways, and a number of bottlers now make a virtue of not chill-filtering their products.

Clearic – *New make* spirit, straight from the still. Clear in colour and high in strength, this was a popular drink with distillery workers when the practice of *dramming* was still extant.

Coffey still – Patented in 1830 by former Irish Inspector-General of Excise Aeneas Coffey, this still revolutionised whisky making. Also known as the *column, continuous* or *patent* still, it allowed large quantities of spirit to be distilled much more quickly than in the traditional *pot still*, paving the way for the development of blended Scotch whisky.

Cutting – During distillation, the stillman, or stillhouse computer programme, 'cuts' from collecting *foreshots* to the *middle cut* or *heart of the run*, before then cutting back to collect *feints*. 'Cut points' are crucial to the character of the spirit produced, and every distillery has its own formula for them, based on alcoholic strength and/or timescale.

Dark grains – Cubes or pellets of high protein animal feed produced by treating *pot ale* with dried *draff*. Pot ale evaporates into a dark brown syrup, hence the name.

Distillation – Distillation follows the process of *fermentation* in whisky making, and is characteristic of all spirit production. During distillation the alcohol is separated from the *wash* by heating it in stills. Alcohol boils at a lower temperature than water and is driven off as vapour, leaving behind the water. It is subsequently condensed back into liquid form.

Draff – The spent *grist* left behind in the *mash tun* after the *mashing* process has been completed. Being high in protein it makes excellent cattle food, and is either sold off to farmers in its 'raw' state or converted into *dark grains*.

Dram – A measure of Scotch whisky of unspecified size. 'Dramming' was the semi-official practice of offering distillery employees amounts of spirit at regular intervals during the working day. The advent of drink driving laws and 'health and safety' legislation finally ended the custom.

Dunnage – Traditional warehousing for whisky *maturation*, which consists of a stone or brick building, ideally with an ash and earth-covered floor. Casks are stacked no more than three high on wooden runners. Most experts believe such warehousing creates the optimum maturation conditions for malt Scotch whisky.

Feints – The final flow of distillation, produced after the *middle cut* has been collected. The feints consist of the heavier compounds and less volatile components of the *low wines*, such as fusel oil. Although not desirable in large quantities, a small amount of feints contributes to the overall character of the whisky being made.

Fermentation – Along with *mashing*, this is part of the *brewing* process of whisky production. Yeast is added to the *wort* in the *washbacks* and the liquid resulting from fermentation is known as *wash*.

Fillings – *New make* spirit, once filled into casks.

Finish – The practice of 'finishing' whisky is a relatively new phenomenon. Essentially, after a substantial period of maturation in its original cask, the whisky is transferred into a different one, which has previously held another alcoholic drink, for a period of finishing. This provides variations on 'house' style. The most common finishes feature various styles of Sherry, but others include rum, Madeira, Burgundy and port.

Foreshots – The initial flow of distillation, produced before the *middle cut* is collected. It contains an excess of acids, aldehydes and esters, but, like *feints*, a small quantity of foreshots contributes to the character of the whisky. As with feints, the amount present depends on the distillery's 'cut points.'

Grain – In Scotland grain whisky is distilled principally from wheat or corn in *continuous* stills. Although a number of single and blended grain whiskies are available, the vast majority of grain whisky distilled is used for blending.

Green malt – At the point when germination is halted during malting, the barley is referred to as green malt.

Grist – Ground, malted barley ready for mashing.

Heart of the run – See *Middle cut*

Hogshead – Often colloquially referred to as a 'hoggie,' the hogshead is a common size of whisky *cask*, having an approximate capacity of 55 gallons (250 litres.)

Kiln – During *malting* the *green malt* is dried in a kiln in order to prevent germination proceeding too far and using up the starch essential for the production of alcohol. Peat smoke may be introduced to flavour the malt, though the principal fuel used in the kiln is coke.

Low wines – In the *pot still* whisky-making process, low wines are the product of the first distillation in the *wash still*. They are impure and weak, and a second distillation in the *spirit* or low wines still is subsequently necessary.

Lyne arm/pipe – also known as a lye arm or lye pipe, this is the pipe connecting the head of the still to the condenser or *worm*. The angle of the lyne arm has a significant effect on the style of spirit produced. See *Reflux*.

Make – The product of a distillery: whisky. See also *New make*.

Malt – Barley, or other grain, prepared for whisky-making by steeping, germinating and kiln-drying. The purpose of malting is to break down the cell walls of the cereal to release the starch and begin the process of converting that into sugars which will subsequently produce alcohol.

Marriage – The practice of vatting whisky prior to bottling in order to achieve a greater degree of harmony. A selection of casks of single malt may be married before bottling, and many blenders marry their blends in a similar fashion.

Mash – *Malt* mixed with hot water to form *wort*. Mashing follows malting and precedes fermentation in the whisky-making process, and the mash of *grist* and hot water is mixed in a large, circular vessel, known as a mash tun. Mashing extracts soluble sugars from the malted grain.

Maturation – Whisky is stored in casks in order to achieve a more mellow and well-rounded spirit, and many countries specify a legal minimum maturation period. During maturation the porous casks allow the whisky to interact with the external atmosphere, and the spirit takes colour and flavour from the wood. At the same time, some of the higher alcohols are transformed into esters and other compounds with attractive aroma and flavour profiles.

Middle cut – The most pure and desirable spirit collected during distillation. Also known as the *Heart of the run*. See *Cutting*.

Moonshine – A term principally used in the USA to denote illicitly-distilled whiskey, often harsh and new. Originally distilled during the hours of darkness using the light of the moon, in order to minimise the chances of detection.

New make – Freshly-distilled whisky. See *Fillings*.

Piece – The term applied to a quantity of germinating *barley* while it is on the malting floor.

Poitin – Irish term for illegally distilled spirit. Often anglicised to 'poteen.'

Pot ale – The high protein waste liquor left in the low wines still after the fist distillation has taken place.

Pot still – A copper distillation vessel. The size and shape of pot stills varies from distillery to distillery, and pot still variables play an important part in determining the character of spirit produced.

Proof – Measurement of the strength of spirits, expressed in degrees, calculated using a hydrometer. Although still employed in the USA, the proof system has now been superseded in Europe by a measurement of alcohol strength as a percentage of alcohol by volume.

Reflux – During distillation some of the heavier flavours with comparatively high boiling points condense from vapour back into liquid form before leaving the still and are subsequently redistilled. This is known as reflux, and the greater the degree of reflux the lighter and 'cleaner' the spirit produced. Short, squat stills produce little reflux, compared to tall, slender stills.

Run – The flow of spirit from a still during a specific period of distillation.

Scotch – Whisky distilled and matured in Scotland, but usually with the colloquial implication of blended whisky.

Silent – Just as a closed theatre is said to be 'dark,' so a closed, though potentially productive, distillery is described as 'silent.'

Single – A single malt whisky is the product of one distillery, not vatted or blended with any others.

Single cask – Most bottles of single malt will contain spirit from between 100 and 150 casks, vatted to give consistency, but a single cask bottling comes from one individual cask. It is frequently sold at cask strength and is prized for its individuality.

Spirit – Until it has been matured for three years in its country of origin, Scotch and Irish whisk(e)y is officially known as spirit.

Spirit safe – A secure, brass and glass box within which *cutting* takes place, without the stillman being able to have direct physical contact with the spirit.

Steep – The vessel in which barley is soaked or steeped during malting.

Still – See *Coffey still* and *Pot still*.

Triple distillation – The practice of distilling whisky three times rather than the usual twice in order to achieve a light, pure style of spirit. Triple distillation is a traditional characteristic of Irish whiskey, and also of Scottish Lowland whisky-making.

Wash – The liquid at the end of the *fermentation* process, ready for distillation.

Washback – The vessel in which fermentation takes place, traditionally constructed of wood, but now often made of stainless steel, which is easier to clean.

Water – One of the key components of whisky production. Water is necessary for steeping during the malting process, for mashing and for cooling the vapour from the stills back into liquid form. As a source of reliable, pure water is crucial to distilling, most distillery sites have been chosen with this in mind.

Wood – Generic term for *casks* used in the whisky industry.

Worm – A long, coiled copper tube, attached to the *lyne arm* of the *pot still*, and fitted into a large wooden vat filled with cold water, known as a worm tub. Before the introduction of 'shell and tube' condensers, the worm tub was the only means of condensing alcohol vapour back into liquid form. A number of distilleries continue to use worm tubs, as experts insist that the character of whisky made using a worm tub differs significantly from that cooled in a modern condenser.

Wort – Essentially unfermented beer, wort is produced in the *mashtun*. See *Mash*.

"Too much of anything is bad, but too much good whiskey is barely enough"
Mark Twain

STATISTICS, CONTACTS
& FESTIVALS

STATISTICS

Some 41,000 Scottish jobs depend on the production of Scotch whisky, accounting for almost two percent of all jobs in Scotland and generating over £800 million of income in Scotland annually. Around 7,000 jobs in remote rural areas of Scotland are supported by the whisky industry, which is Scotland's second largest export earning industry (after electronics). It is the UK's fifth largest export earning industry (after chemicals, metal goods, textiles and office equipment), and whisky exports have exceeded £2 billion for each of the past twelve years. In 2005 they stood at £2.36 billion.

During that year, 82.5 million cases of Scotch whisky were sold worldwide. Laid end to end they would stretch 17,437 miles, or three times the distance between Edinburgh and Shanghai. In total, 31 bottles were sold overseas each second. Remarkably, exports were worth £252,674 per employee, while tax to the UK Treasury from Scotch whisky companies amounted to £85,561 for each employee.

The Greeks drink more Scotch whisky per person than any other nationality, while a greater quantity of Scotch is sold in one month in France than Cognac in an entire year. Scotch whisky is sold in over 200 markets around the world, and some 18.5 million casks are currently maturing in Scottish warehouses.

UK taxation on a typical bottle of blended Scotch whisky:

Excise duty	5.48
VAT	1.59
Total tax (66%)	7.07
Scotch whisky (34%)	3.63
Cost to the consumer	**£10.70**

In the USA, 14.3 million nine-litre cases of Bourbon were sold during 2005, generating over $1.5 billion in revenue for distillers. According to the Distilled Spirits Council of the United States' Economic & Strategic Development Department, "Bourbon's increasing popularity in overseas markets has allowed exports to grow to almost $40 million in 2005."

CONTACTS

SCOTLAND

The Scotch Whisky Association is the guardian of Scotch whisky, protecting its authenticity and reputation all over the world, and its website offers a great deal of essential information on the subject of Scotch. See **www.scotch-whisky.org.uk**

The Scotch Malt Whisky Society bottles single cask whiskies exclusively for its members and hosts whisky-related events in a number of countries. Tel: + 44 (0) 131 555 2929 or visit **www.smws.com**

Scotland's Malt Whisky Trail currently encompasses seven Speyside distilleries which are open to the public, along with the historic Dallas Dhu Distillery (in the care of Historic Scotland) and the Speyside Cooperage, where the visitor can watch coopers practising their ancient art. See **www.maltwhiskytrail.com**

An ideal Scottish starting point for the comparative novice is the Scotch Whisky Heritage Centre, located close to Edinburgh Castle. 354 Castlehill, Edinburgh. Tel: +44 (0) 131 2200441 **www.whisky-heritage.co.uk**

www.scotlandwhisky.com is an independent one-stop shop for the visitor to Scotland with an interest in Scotch whisky, offering a wide range of consumer information. As the website says, "Use scotlandwhisky to book your visit, locate your nearest distillery and find the most direct route to Scotland - See the country, taste the spirit."

IRELAND

In addition to the visitor centres at Ireland's working distilleries of Bushmills, Cooley and Midleton, there are a number of other interesting whiskey-related heritage sites in the country. These include Locke's Distillery Museum is at Kilbeggan in County Westmeath (Tel: + 353 0506 32134), **www.lockesdistillerymuseum.com**, while the Tullamore Dew Heritage Centre is at Bury Quay, Tullamore, County Offaly (Tel: +353 5793 25015), **www.tullamore-dew.org**. The Irish Whiskey Heritage Centre is located in the Old Jameson Distillery, Bow Street, Smithfield, Dublin D7 (Tel: +353 1807 2355, **www.jamesonwhiskey.com**

www.classicwhiskey.com is a commercial site geared to the sale of Irish whiskey, but it also boasts informative sections devoted to the history and production of Irish whiskey, along with many useful links.

USA

To discover more about whiskey in the USA visit **www.americanwhiskeytrail.com**, which links to relevant historical sites, including the fascinating Oscar Goetz Museum in Bardstown, Kentucky and the reconstruction of George Washington's distillery at Mount Vernon in Virginia (see p67). It also links to the nine US distilleries which welcome visitors. See also **www.kybourbonfestival.com** and **www.visitbardstown.com**

CANADA

A number of Canadian distilleries are open to the public, along with the Seagram Museum, 57 Erb Street West, Waterloo, Ontario N2L 6C2 – **www.seagram-museum.ca**

AUSTRALIA

Tasmania Distillery Museum, 2 Maquarie St, Hobart, Tasmania 7000 – **www.tasdistillery.com.au**

JAPAN

Suntory operates visitor centres at its Hakushu and Yamazaki distilleries – **www.suntory.ja**

Nikka Whisky Museum – **www.nikka.com/topics/whisky museum**

OTHER USEFUL CONTACTS

European Confederation of Spirits Producers – **www.europeanspirits.org**
Distilled Spirits Council of the United States – **www.discus.org**

Association of Canadian Distillers –
www.canadiandistillers.com
Distilled Spirits Association of New Zealand –
www.distillers.co.nz

Whisky Magazine (**www.whiskymag.com**) and Malt
Advocate (**www.maltadvocate.com**) are the two
principal specialist English language whisky periodicals,
while for an all-round generic whisky-related website
which covers the subject on an authoritative, global basis
and boasts regular updates visit **www.whisky-
pages.com** The more obsessive whisky enthusiast will
find much to interest him at **www.maltmadness.com**

FESTIVALS

FEBRUARY

Münchner Whisky Festival,
Praterinsel, Munich, Germany
www.whisky-festival.de

North Netherlands Whisky Festival,
Martiniplaza, Groningen, Netherlands
www.wfnn.nl

Whisky Live Tokyo, Tokyo Big Sight, Tokyo, Japan
www.whiskylive.com/japan

International Malt Whisky Festival,
La Tentation, Brussels, Belgium
www.whiskyfestival.be

MARCH

Whisky Live London,
The Lawrence Hall & Conference Centre,

The Royal Horticultural Halls, London, England
www.whiskylive.com/england

**Binny's Annual 'Whiskeys of the
World Expo',**
Binny's in Lakeview, 3000 N Clark, Chicago, USA
www.binnys.com

APRIL

Whisky Messen,
Bramdrupham Hallerne, Kolding, Denmark
www.whiskymessen.dk

Whisky Live New York,
Tavern On The Green, Central Park West,
New York, USA
www.whiskylive.com/usa/newyork

The Whisky Fair Limburg,
Josef-Kohlmaier-Halle, Limburg, Germany
www.whiskyfair.com

Whisky Live Lille,
Couvent des Minimes, Alliance Lille, Lille, France
www.whisky.fr

Whisky Fest Chicago,
Hyatt Regency on Wacker Drive, Chicago, USA
www.maltadvocate.com

Whiskies of the World Expo – San Francisco,
Palace Hotel, San Francisco, USA
www.celticmalts.com

MAY

The Spirit of Speyside Whisky Festival,
Speyside, Scotland www.dufftown.co.uk and
www.spiritofspeyside.com (Spirit of Speyside Whisky
Festival Limited, PO Box 4, Aberlour AB38 9WZ).

Whisky Festival Greece,
City Hotel, Thessaloniki, Greece

Madrid Whisky Fair,
Madrid, Spain

Feis Ile – The Islay Festival of Malt and Music,
Islay, Scotland
www.feisile.org

AUGUST

Royal Mile Whiskies 'Whisky Fringe',
Mansfield Traquair, Edinburgh, Scotland
www.royalmilewhiskies.com

SEPTEMBER

Whisky Live Glasgow,
George Square, Glasgow, Scotland
www.whiskylive.com/scotland

Cöpenicker Whiskyherbst,
Berlin, Germany
www.whisky-herbst.de

Whisky Live Paris,
Palais Brogniart, Paris, France
www.whiskylive.com/france

The Autumn Scotch Whisky Festival
Dufftown, Speyside, Scotland
www.dufftown.co.uk

OCTOBER

Smak av Whisky (Malmö Whisky Fair),
Slagthuset, Malmö, Sweden
www.smakavwhisky.se

Milano Whisky Festival,
Hotel Marriot, Via Washington 66, Milano, Italy
www.whiskyfestival.it

NOVEMBER

Whisky Fest New York,
Marriot Marquis, Times Square, New York, USA
www.maltadvocate.com

International Whisky Fair,
Pieterskerk, Leiden, Netherlands
www.whiskyfestival.nl

DECEMBER

Whisky Ship,
Zurich, Switzerland
www.whiskyship.ch

SELECT BIBLIOGRAPHY

Broom, Dave:
Handbook of Whisky. Hamlyn. 2000.
Graham, Duncan & Wendy:
Visiting Distilleries.
Neil Wilson Publishing, 2nd edition 2003
Jackson, Michael:
Michael Jackson's Malt Whisky Companion.
Dorling Kindersley, 5th edition, 2004
Jackson, Michael:
Whisky - The Definitive World Guide,
Dorling Kindersley, 2005
McDougall, John and **Smith, Gavin D**:
Worts, Worms & Washbacks.
Angels' Share. 1999.
MacLean, Charles:
MacLean's Miscellany of Whisky.
Little Books. 2004.
MacLean, Charles:
Scotch Whisky.
Pitkin. 1996.
Mulryan, Peter:
The Whiskeys of Ireland.
O'Brian Press. 2002.
Murray, Jim:
Classic Blended Scotch.
Prion Books. 1999.
Murray, Jim:
Classic Bourbon, Tennessee and Rye Whiskey.
Prior Books. 1998.
Murray, Jim:
Classic Irish Whiskey.
Prion Books. 1997.
Ronde, Ingvar (ed):
Malt Whisky Yearbook 2007